W9-BAI-374

WORLD ALMANAC
LIBRARY OF THE STATES

Massachusetts

THE BAY STATE

by Rachel Barenblat

Curriculum Consultant: Jean Craven,
Director of Instructional Support,
Albuquerque, NM, Public Schools

WORLD ALMANAC® LIBRARY

Please visit our web site at: www.worldalmanaclibrary.com
For a free color catalog describing World Almanac® Library's list of high-quality books
and multimedia programs, call 1-800-848-2928 or fax your request to (414) 332-3567.

Library of Congress Cataloging-in-Publication Data

Barenblat, Rachel.
    Massachusetts, the Bay State / by Rachel Barenblat.
        p. cm. — (World Almanac Library of the states)
    Includes bibliographical references and index.
    Summary: Illustrations and text present the history, geography, people, politics and
government, economy, and social life and customs of Massachusetts, home to Plymouth
Rock and the Basketball Hall of Fame.
    ISBN 0-8368-5123-4 (lib. bdg.)
    ISBN 0-8368-5286-9 (softcover)
    1. Massachusetts—Juvenile literature. [1. Massachusetts.] I. Title. II. Series.
F64.3.B47   2002
974.4—dc21   2001046996

This edition first published in 2002 by
World Almanac® Library
330 West Olive Street, Suite 100
Milwaukee, WI 53212 USA

This edition © 2002 by World Almanac® Library.

Design and Editorial: **Jack&Bill**/Bill SMITH STUDIO Inc.
Editors: Jackie Ball and Kristen Behrens
Art Directors: Ron Leighton and Jeffrey Rutzky
Photo Research and Buying: Christie Silver and Sean Livingstone
Design and Production: Maureen O'Connor and Jeffrey Rutzky
World Almanac® Library Editors: Patricia Lantier, Amy Stone, Valerie J. Weber,
Catherine Gardner, Carolyn Kott Washburne, Alan Wachtel, Monica Rausch
World Almanac® Library Production: Scott M. Krall, Eva Erato-Rudek, Tammy Gruenewald,
Katherine A. Goedheer

Photo credits: p. 5 © PhotoDisc; p. 6 © PhotoDisc (left); p. 6 (top right) © Corel; p. 6 (bottom
right) © Corel; p. 7 (top), (bottom) © Corel; p. 9 © Corel; p. 10 © Corel; p. 11 © ArtToday;
p. 12 © Corel; p. 13 © Corel; p. 14 © Bettmann/CORBIS; p. 15 © Corel; p. 17 © Corel; p. 18
© PhotoDisc; p. 19 © Corel; p. 20 © Painet, © Painet, © PhotoDisc; p. 21 © Painet, © Mark E.
Gibson/CORBIS, © Corel; p. 23 © Corel; p. 26 (top) © Jeffrey L. Rotman/CORBIS; p. 26 (bottom)
© Library of Congress; p. 27 © Corel; p. 29 © Corel; p. 30 © Corel; p. 31 (all) © Library of
Congress; p. 32 © ArtToday; p. 33 © Corel; p. 34 © Corel; p. 35 © Jim Bourg/TimePix; p. 36
© Library of Congress; p. 37 © Dover Publications; p. 38 © ArtToday; p. 39 © ArtToday; p. 40
© ArtToday; p. 41 © Library of Congress; p. 42 © Library of Congress; p. 44 (top left) © Artville;
p. 44 (bottom left) © PhotoDisc; p. 44 (bottom right) © PhotoDisc; p. 45 © PhotoDisc

Printed in the United States of America

1 2 3 4 5 6 7 8 9 06 05 04 03 02

Massachusetts

INTRODUCTION	4
ALMANAC	6
HISTORY	8
THE PEOPLE	16
THE LAND	20
ECONOMY & COMMERCE	24
POLITICS & GOVERNMENT	28
CULTURE & LIFESTYLE	32
NOTABLE PEOPLE	38
TIME LINE	42
STATE EVENTS & ATTRACTIONS	44
MORE ABOUT MASSACHUSETTS	46
INDEX	47

Past and Future

The history of Massachusetts is the history of America. It was there that the Pilgrims and Puritans established their historic colonies and the first Thanksgiving feast was held. The first college in the United States, Harvard, was founded in Massachusetts. The Revolutionary War began in Massachusetts; when the Industrial Revolution leaped across the Atlantic, it started its U.S. life on Massachusetts soil.

Although it is a small state, Massachusetts includes more than 1,000 miles (1,609 kilometers) of rugged coastline, fertile river valleys, and gentle mountain ranges that stretch into neighboring states. Most of the state's inhabitants live in cities; the state capital, Boston, is considered one of the country's friendliest and most striking urban areas. Massachusetts is also home to beautiful small towns, many of which are becoming revitalized as the computer/Internet economy brings new jobs to their abandoned mills.

Massachusetts is filled with exciting people and picturesque places. Cape Cod and its offshore islands are marked by weathered gray cedar shingle houses and bright red cranberry bogs, while Boston is home to historic Back Bay and hip shopping areas such as Newbury Street and Harvard Square. Central Massachusetts is checkered with farms and fields, and the western part of the state rolls with hills that look purple as the sun sets.

Massachusetts is known as "The Bay State," after the body of water framed by the curve of Cape Cod's "arm." In the state's early days, the sea was the source of new enterprises and new adventures. Today those adventures may come in the form of business, sports, computers, or the arts. All of these and more can be found within Massachusetts's borders.

Massachusetts may be rich with history and the past, but it is also a great place to seek the American future.

▶ Map of Massachusetts showing interstate highway system, as well as major cities and waterways.

▶ A misty waterfront on Cape Ann, one of Massachusetts's charming coastal areas.

MASSACHUSETTS

VERMONT

NEW HAMPSHIRE

ATLANTIC OCEAN

N

Schenectady
Troy
Albany

NEW YORK

Nashua

Merrimack R.

Lowell

91

Pittsfield

190

290

495

Waltham
Brookline
Cambridge
Boston
Quincy

Massachusetts Bay

Great Barrington

Worcester

Framingham

Charles R.

93

Weymouth
Brockton

Chicopee
Springfield

84

395

90

95

495

Plymouth

Cape Cod Bay

Pawtucket
Providence

Cranston
Warwick

95

East Hartford
New Britain

CONNECTICUT

RHODE ISLAND

Fall River

195

New Bedford

Buzzards Bay

Hyannis

Nantucket Sound

Martha's Vineyard

Gardiners Bay

Rhode Island Sound

Nantucket Island

SCALE/KEY

0   50 Miles

0   50 Kilometers

⭐ Capital

---·--- State Border

🛣87 Interstate Highways

MASSACHUSETTS 5

Fast Facts

MASSACHUSETTS (MA), The Bay State

Entered Union

February 6, 1788 (6th state)

Capital   **Population**

Boston 589,141

Total Population (2000)

6,349,097 (13th most populous state)

Largest Cities   **Population**

Boston 589,141
Worcester 172,648
Springfield 152,082
Lowell 105,167

Land Area

7,840 square miles (20,306 square
kilometers) (45th largest state)

State Motto

Ense petit placidam sub libertate
quietem *(By the sword we seek peace,
but peace only under liberty)*

State Song

"All Hail to Massachusetts" *by Arthur
Marsh*

State Cat

Tabby cat

State Dog

Boston terrier — *A cross
between the English bulldog
and the English terrier,
this was the first purebred
dog developed in the U.S.*

State Bird

Black-capped chickadee

State Fish

Cod

State Insect

Ladybug

State Tree

American elm — *There are very few
American elm trees left in the United
States today as they are prone to a
fungus that eventually kills them.*

State Flower

Mayflower

State Berry

Cranberry — *There are
three cultivated fruits
native to North America:
the blueberry, the cranberry,
and the Concord grape.*

State Beverage

Cranberry juice — *A glass of
cranberry juice can provide more than
100 percent of the recommended daily
allowance of Vitamin C, which helps
the human body absorb iron and fight
infections.*

State Muffin

Corn muffin

State Dessert

Boston Cream Pie

State Cookie

Chocolate-chip cookie —
*This cookie was invented in
1930 at the Tollhouse
Restaurant in Whitman.*

PLACES TO VISIT

Cape Cod National Seashore
This 40-mile (64-km) ribbon of land along the Cape Cod coast, set aside in 1961 as a national seashore, has hiking and biking trails, beaches, and picnic areas. It is also a regular stopover for more than three hundred species of gulls, terns, ducks, geese, and swans.

The Freedom Trail
This historical walk through Boston includes Boston Common, the old and new state houses, Park Street Church, the Old Granary Burying Ground, Old Corner Bookstore, Faneuil Hall, Paul Revere House, the Old North Church, and the battleship USS *Constitution,* better known as Old Ironsides.

Mount Greylock State Reservation
At 3,491 feet (1,064 meters), Mt. Greylock is the highest peak in Massachusetts. For years Mt. Greylock has inspired artists and writers, including Herman Melville and Henry David Thoreau. At the summit visitors can see a panorama of five states.

For other places and events to attend, see p. 44.

BIGGEST, BEST, AND MOST

- Sterling was home to Mary Sawyer Tyler (1806–1899), whose claim to fame is that her pet lamb, Nathaniel, followed her to school one day. Someone even wrote a song about it.

- The "World's Biggest World" — the largest rotating globe — can be found in Wellesley. It weighs 25 tons and is 28 feet (7 m) in diameter.

- With the Massachusetts Institute of Technology (MIT) located in Cambridge, it is not surprising that the town is home to more than forty Nobel Prize Winners.

STATE FIRSTS

- In 1638, Stephen Daye established the first printing press in America.
- In 1775, the first battles of the Revolutionary War were fought at Lexington and Concord.

Cookie Capital?

Not only is Massachusetts the birthplace of the Tollhouse chocolate-chip cookie, but of Fig Newtons, too. The cookie was invented in Cambridge, where the manager of the Kennedy Biscuit Works decided to name it after a Massachusetts town. "Cambridges" was too much of a mouthful, so the manager held a contest and nearby "Newton" won. Later, the name was extended to "Fig Newton" after the company was bought by the National Biscuit Company, better known today as Nabisco.

Plymouth, Virginia?

The history of Massachusetts might have been very different if the Pilgrims had actually arrived at the destination for which they set sail. The *Mayflower* left port from Plymouth, England, on September 16, 1620, and set a course for Virginia. The Pilgrims landed at Plymouth Rock only because a storm blew the *Mayflower* off course. They eventually landed at Plymouth Harbor after three months of travel, on December 21, more than 300 miles (483 km) farther north than they had intended.

▼ **The Billings Landing protects Plymouth Rock.**

The Land "Near the Great Hill"

> Whilst we were busied hereabout, there presented himself a savage called Samoset, which caused alarm . . . He saluted us in English, and bade us welcome, for he had learned some broken English among the Englishmen that came to fish at Monhegan Island . . . he was stark naked, only a leather about his waist, with a fringe . . .
>
> — *Diary of a Pilgrim, March 16, 1621*

The earliest inhabitants of what is now Massachusetts were Native Americans who migrated into this part of the country ten thousand years ago. They hunted mastodons, mammoths, and caribou for meat and made tools from rocks and bones.

As the climate grew warmer, forests began to grow. Other people arrived, who hunted deer and turkeys and fished for cod. They gathered wild strawberries and planted corn, beans, and squash. They quarried soapstone and carved it into cooking pots and made dugout canoes from tree trunks.

Over time seven different Native American tribes came to call the Massachusetts region their home. All of these tribes spoke Algonquian. They moved with the seasons among several village sites. The staple of their diet was corn; some tribes also cultivated beans. They all fished and hunted.

The First Europeans

> *After many difficulties in boisterous storms, by God's providence, by break of day we espied land which we deemed to be Cape Cod . . .*
> — Journal of an early English settler, November 9, 1620

Historians are not exactly sure when the first Europeans came to Massachusetts. Leif Eriksson, a Norseman, may have set foot on Cape Cod in 1003. In 1605 the region was mapped by French explorer Samuel de Champlain. In 1614, Captain John Smith, of the Virginia Colony, mapped the New England coast.

Native Americans of Massachusetts
Massachuset
Mohican
Nauset
Nipmuc
Pennacook
Pocumtuc
Wampanoag

DID YOU KNOW?

The state name *Massachusetts* comes from the Massachuset tribe and means "large hill place" or "near the great hill."

DID YOU KNOW?

The first lighthouse in the United States was built in Boston in 1716.

The Plymouth Colony

*Being thus arrived in a good harbor, and brought safe to
land, they fell upon their knees and blessed the God of
heaven who had brought them over the vast and furious
ocean, again to set their feet on the firm and stable earth.*
— Journal of Governor William Bradford, 1620

▲ Asher Brown Durand
painted the scenery
at Monument
Mountain, in the
Berkshires.

In England a group of people who disagreed with the Church
of England wanted to form their own church. They became
known as Separatists. A group of Separatists sailed on the
Mayflower bound for North America on September 16, 1620.

Before landing, forty-one of the men on the ship agreed
to make their own laws for the new colony. They wrote a
document called the Mayflower Compact, the first document
in U.S. history to establish the idea of government by the
people, "for the general good" of the people.

The Separatists landed in December 1620 and called their
new village Plymouth after the port from which they had
sailed. Their first governor, William Bradford, called their
band "Pilgrims." Only about half of them survived that first
winter. When spring came the Pilgrims began to plant. The
Wampanoag shared native seeds with the settlers and taught
them how to use fish as fertilizer for their crops.

The Wampanoag chief, Massasoit, made a peace treaty with the English that was observed until his death. It was the Wampanoag who celebrated the "First Thanksgiving" with the Pilgrims; the meal included venison, geese, turkey, chowder, oysters, lobsters, fruit, biscuits, Indian pudding, and popcorn balls.

The Massachusetts Bay Colony

In 1630 the *Arbella* sailed into Massachusetts Bay with one thousand colonists on board. These colonists called themselves Puritans. John Winthrop was their leader in matters both spiritual and practical.

Unlike the Pilgrims, the Puritans did not want to break away from the Church of England. They just wanted to change some church practices. They wanted to worship in their own way, but they also wanted everyone within their colony to follow Puritan rules. There was no separation of church and state, and no freedom of religion, within the Massachusetts Bay Colony.

Colony Changes

In 1691 Plymouth became part of the Massachusetts Bay Colony. The new colony then included coastal lands that stretched as far as modern-day Maine.

Colonial News

"It is designed, that the Countrey shall be furnished once a month (or if any Glut of Occurrences happen, oftener) with an Account of such considerable things as have arrived unto our Notice. In order here unto, the Publisher will take what pains he can to obtain a Faithful Relation of all such things . . ." So began the first edition of *Publick Occurrences both Forreign and Domestick*, the first colonial newspaper, printed in Boston on September 25, 1690. The issue reported on missing children from the town of Chelmsford, the waning smallpox epidemic in Boston, a recent Boston fire, fighting with various Native American tribes, and news about a planned possible expedition into Canada.

◀ A replica of the *Mayflower,* the boat in which Pilgrims sailed to Plymouth in 1620.

Ship owners made fortunes sailing in the "Triangle Trade." In Massachusetts and other New England colonies, ships left for West Africa loaded with rum and other goods to trade for African slaves. From Africa, the ships sailed for the West Indies and the southern colonies to sell the slaves to plantation owners. There the ships were loaded with goods such as cotton, sugar, tobacco, and molasses and sailed back to New England, where the sugar and molasses were used to make rum for export.

The English felt that the main purpose of the American colonies was to provide resources for the British Empire. They wanted all products grown or manufactured in the colonies to come to England; they wanted all goods sold in the colonies, no matter where they came from, to be carried on English ships. The colonists did not agree with these viewpoints. This disagreement was a major cause of the Revolutionary War.

The Road to Revolution

Taxes equally detrimental to the Commercial interests of the Parent Country and her Colonies, are imposed upon the People, without their Consent . . .
— Letter from John Hancock, Joseph Jackson, John Ruddock, John Rowe and Samuel Pemberton, Selectmen of Boston, September 14, 1768.

By the 1760s Britain controlled most of eastern North America. More and more colonists, however, were beginning to feel separate from the mother country.

In 1764 the British Parliament passed the Sugar Act, which placed a tax on molasses entering the colonies from ports outside the British Empire. The next year the Stamp Act levied taxes on newspapers, legal documents, and even playing cards, and the Townshend Acts of 1767 taxed tea and other items.

Many colonists opposed these taxes, and fights broke out between colonists and British soldiers stationed in Boston. During one of these

Deborah Samson
1760–1827

Deborah Samson was born in Winnetuxet (now Plymouth) and by age ten was an indentured servant who worked in the fields and the house of a minister, Deacon Thomas, also learning to hunt with a musket for food. Her servitude ended at age eighteen and she became a schoolteacher. In 1780 she learned from Thomas that his two sons had been killed in the Revolutionary War. Two years later, at the age of twenty-one, she enlisted for three years in the Fourth Massachusetts Regiment as Robert Shurtleff. Her deception went unnoticed as she fought in several battles, but finally her luck ran out. A Philadelphia doctor discovered her deception and revealed it to her commanding officer. The officer sent "Shurtleff," along with a letter, to General George Washington. Upon learning that she was a woman, General Washington gave her an honorable discharge and money to return home. In 1804 she became the first woman to receive a military pension from the U.S. government. In 1983 she became the official State Heroine of Massachusetts.

fights, on March 5, 1770, five colonists were killed. Colonial leaders labeled the fight the "Boston Massacre" to drive anti-British sentiments among the colonists.

In 1773 Parliament passed a new law that gave the British East India Company a monopoly on the sale of tea in the American colonies. In protest Colonial activist Samuel Adams and his friends raided British ships in Boston Harbor and dumped their cargo overboard; Parliament retaliated by closing the port of Boston and passing what some colonists called the Intolerable Acts. The incident became known as the Boston Tea Party.

Continental Congress

Many colonists were shocked at Parliament's reaction to the Boston tea protests. The legislature of the colony of Virginia proposed that all the colonies meet to decide what to do.

All of the colonies except Georgia sent delegates to the First Continental Congress, which opened in Philadelphia on September 5, 1774. Four of the fifty-six delegates were from Massachusetts, including cousins Samuel and John Adams. The Congress decided to ask Parliament to repeal

▼ The Battle of Bunker Hill was one of the first battles of the American Revolution.

the Intolerable Acts, and the delegates also agreed to boycott trade with Great Britain until Parliament listened.

The next year, as tensions grew, British troops in Boston were ordered to seize weapons held by colonial militias; when word of that order reached Samuel Adams and his friends, they sent Paul Revere and William Dawes out to warn the countryside that the British were coming. Fighting between British soldiers and colonists broke out on April 19, 1775, in the towns of Lexington and Concord. A few weeks later the Continental Congress met again; they chose George Washington, a planter from Virginia, to lead their new army.

At least one-third of the colonists in North America were opposed to separation from Great Britain. These people were called Tories, or Loyalists. Many of them left, mostly for Canada.

On June 17, 1775, one of the first major battles of the Revolutionary War was fought across the Charles River from Boston. The British won the battle of Bunker Hill, but almost half of their soldiers (called Redcoats for their bright uniforms) were killed or wounded.

▲ The Boston Tea Party Museum.

A Nation Is Born

We hold these truths to be self-evident, that all men are created equal, that they are endowed by their Creator with certain unalienable Rights, that among these are Life, Liberty, and the pursuit of Happiness . . .
— The Declaration of Independence

The Continental Congress adopted the Declaration of Independence on July 4, 1776. Boston native Benjamin Franklin convinced France to help the colonies; later he and John Adams were two of the negotiators of the Treaty of Paris, which ended the Revolutionary War in 1783 and established American independence.

Massachusetts was the sixth state to ratify the U.S. Constitution, on February 6, 1788. Four months later the constitution was ratified by the nine states required to bring it into force.

Other Revolutions

In 1810 a merchant named Francis Cabot Lowell visited Manchester, England, an industrial city filled with textile mills. Lowell memorized how the machinery worked. In 1814 Lowell opened the first power loom factory in America.

Lowell died in 1817, but he had brought the Industrial Revolution to Massachusetts. Throughout the nineteenth century manufacturing grew by leaps and bounds. Textile, shoe, and paper industries were at the forefront of that growth explosion.

Shipping, shipbuilding, and whaling also contributed to Massachusetts's prosperity. Donald MacKay in Boston became the foremost builder of a new, fast type of ship called a Clipper.

Slavery had been illegal in Massachusetts since 1783. By 1790 there were no slaves in the state; in the early 1800s, Bostonian William Lloyd Garrison began publishing

▼ Students at Mt. Holyoke supplemented studies with lessons in baseball in the early 1900s.

The Liberator, an abolitionist newspaper. Garrison was also an advocate of women's suffrage. In 1850 Worcester hosted the first national Women's Rights Convention. The theme was liberation.

More than 150,000 men from Massachusetts served in the Union forces during the Civil War (1861–1865). The 54th Massachusetts Volunteer Infantry was the nation's first African-American regiment; it was led by Boston abolitionist Colonel Robert Gould Shaw.

▲ The Robert Gould Shaw Memorial and 54th Regiment Memorial. The 54th was the first African-American regiment to be recruited in the North in the effort to muster troops for the Civil War.

The Twentieth Century

In 1900 approximately 2.5 million people lived in Massachusetts. Brothers Francis and Freelan Stanley manufactured the Stanley Steamer, a steam-powered automobile, in Massachusetts from 1897 to 1924. Traffic in Boston became so bad that the nation's first subway was opened beneath Boston Common.

Over time manufacturing shifted to southern and western states, where land and workers were cheaper. This led to difficult economic times for Massachusetts. The state began unemployment programs in 1929, at the start of the Great Depression.

World War II brought an economic boom to Massachusetts. Factories and shipyards produced supplies for the war. Electronics and communications industries, which began to thrive after World War II, helped the Massachusetts economy get back on its feet.

In the 1960s civil rights struggles affected Massachusetts. In 1972 a group of Boston African-American parents and the National Association for the Advancement of Colored People (NAACP) went to federal district court because few Boston schools were racially integrated. In 1974 a judge declared that the schools were "unconstitutionally segregated," and efforts were made to integrate the schools by busing children from one part of the city to another.

New World, New Beginnings

> Other countries depend upon the multiplication of their own native people. This country is constantly drinking strength out of new sources by the voluntary association with it of great bodies of strong men and forward-looking women. And so by the gift of the free will of independent people it is constantly being renewed from generation to generation by the same process by which it was originally created.
>
> — *Woodrow Wilson, "Americanism and the Foreign-Born," May 1915*

Although the first inhabitants of Massachusetts were Native Americans and, later, English settlers, today Massachusetts's more than six million residents come from every ethnic background imaginable.

The 1600s brought English settlers to Massachusetts. Until it was abolished in the late 1700s, the slave trade brought Africans. Descendants of both these groups continue to live in Massachusetts today.

The Industrial Revolution created a great change in the ethnic makeup of Massachusetts. As more and more mills were built in the 1800s, Irish immigrants came there to work. The work was difficult and pay was low, but the immigrants were willing to put up with terrible conditions

Age Distribution in Massachusetts

0–4	397,268
5–19	1,278,025
20–24	404,279
25–44	1,989,783
45–64	1,419,760
65 and over	860,162

Patterns of Immigration

The total number of people who immigrated to Massachusetts in 1998 was 15,869. Of that number, the largest immigrant groups were from China (9%), the Dominican Republic (7%), and Haiti (7%).

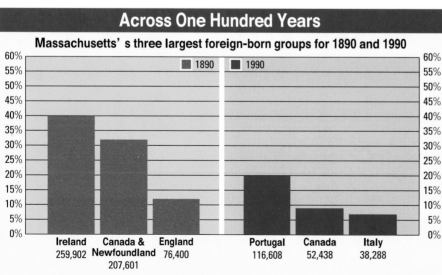

Across One Hundred Years

Massachusetts' s three largest foreign-born groups for 1890 and 1990

■ 1890 ■ 1990

Ireland 259,902 Canada & Newfoundland 207,601 England 76,400

Portugal 116,608 Canada 52,438 Italy 38,288

Total state population: 2,238,943
Total foreign-born: 657,137 (29%)

Total state population: 6,016,425
Total foreign-born: 573,733 (10%)

because it allowed them to "get their start" in the United States.

In the early twentieth century, Italians were the largest immigrant group entering the state. Irish, English, and Italian are still the top three ancestries in Massachusetts

▲ Quincy Market in Boston attracts crowds of shoppers, diners, and strollers every summer.

Heritage and Background of Massachusetts Residents — Year 2000

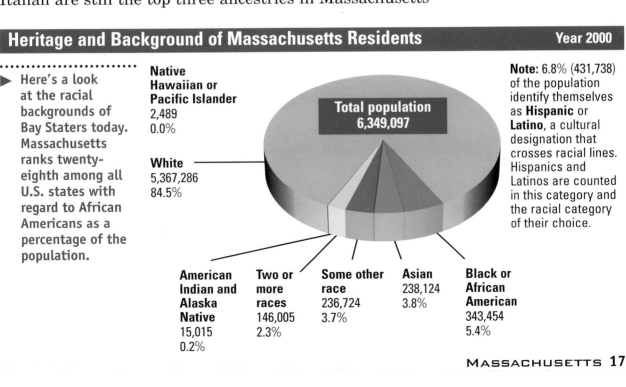

▶ Here's a look at the racial backgrounds of Bay Staters today. Massachusetts ranks twenty-eighth among all U.S. states with regard to African Americans as a percentage of the population.

Native Hawaiian or Pacific Islander
2,489
0.0%

White
5,367,286
84.5%

Total population 6,349,097

Note: 6.8% (431,738) of the population identify themselves as **Hispanic** or **Latino**, a cultural designation that crosses racial lines. Hispanics and Latinos are counted in this category and the racial category of their choice.

American Indian and Alaska Native
15,015
0.2%

Two or more races
146,005
2.3%

Some other race
236,724
3.7%

Asian
238,124
3.8%

Black or African American
343,454
5.4%

— 26 percent claim Irish descent, 15 percent English descent, and 14 percent Italian descent.

In the last thirty or forty years, many immigrants to Massachusetts have been Spanish-speaking, from Cuba, Puerto Rico, the Dominican Republic, and elsewhere. Almost 7 percent of Massachusetts residents have Latino ancestry.

Massachusetts is also home to people of Polish, Canadian, Chinese, French, Greek, German, Scandinavian, Syrian, Southeast Asian, and other ancestry. Many people of Portuguese ancestry live in and around Fall River and New

Educational Levels of Massachusetts Residents	
Less than 9th grade	317,943
9th to 12th grade, no diploma	474,714
High school graduate, including equivalency	1,178,509
Some college, no degree or associate's degree	909,058
Bachelor's degree	657,161
Graduate or professional degree	421,838

▼ The city of Boston sits across the Charles River from Cambridge.

Bedford. Many African Americans live in Boston, Cambridge, Roxbury, and Dorchester (in the eastern part of the state), and Springfield (in the west).

Few Native Americans remain in Massachusetts, despite the prevalence of Native place-names.

Ninety-six percent of Massachusetts residents live in urban areas. Only three other states in the nation have a higher percentage of urban dwellers.

About 26 percent of the population over the age of three is enrolled in school, making Massachusetts thirty-fifth in the nation in school enrollment. Just under 1 percent of the state's inhabitants work as teachers.

Religion

Although Massachusetts began as a Protestant state (both the Pilgrims and the Puritans came mainly for religious reasons), it now has many Roman Catholics. Some towns have so many Catholic residents that there are separate Roman Catholic churches frequented by Catholics of different ethnicities (usually Irish Catholics, Polish Catholics, and Italian Catholics).

The Puritan Congregational Church was the state's official church until an amendment to the state constitution was passed in 1833 ending state affiliation with any church. Even today churches are often found in the most prominent areas of towns and villages because they have traditionally played a great role in social life.

The majority of people who live in Massachusetts and are affiliated with a religion are Protestant Christians of various kinds, but nearly one third of the population is Catholic. Among the Protestant churches represented in the state are Methodists, Episcopalians, Presbyterians, and Quakers. Just over 4 percent of the population are Jewish, and 1 percent are agnostic.

▲ Bostonians celebrate their many different ethnic heritages with colorful street festivals.

From Mountains to Coast

> The geologic story of the Woods Hole area was written by glacial ice during the last ice age and edited by the ocean waves. If you learn to read today's landscape, you can see the fascinating history it records. The features of Cape Cod, from the ponds and cranberry bogs to the gently sloping sandy uplands and rocky, irregular hills to the beaches, result from the glacial processes that built the cape and the marine processes that still shape it.
>
> — *Deborah Hutchinson and Beth Schwarzman, 2001*

Massachusetts has a land area of 7,840 square miles (20,306 sq km), the forty-fifth largest of any state in the union. The coastline is about 1,500 miles (2,414 km) long, even though the state measures only 190 miles (306 km) from east to west and 110 miles (177 km) from north to south.

The Massachusetts coast was formed centuries ago by glaciers. When the ice melted, roughly eleven thousand years ago, the rocky shoreline was exposed. Near the center of the state, the glaciers left stony pastures; in the west the terrain rolls with gentle hills.

Massachusetts has two major regions — the Coastal Lowlands and New England Upland. The Upland is divided into the Connecticut River Valley and the Berkshires.

Coastal Lowlands

More than one-third of the state is considered Coastal

▼ *From left to right:* **Beverly Pond; Plum Island National Wildlife Refuge; Cape Cod; a road near Sturbridge Village; Mount Greylock; a red fox kit.**

Lowland, extending inland from the ocean. This is a region of low hills and many swamps, lakes, rivers, and ponds. Most of the soil is too rocky for farming, although one crop, cranberries, does grow well there.

At the far end of the lowlands is the feature that gives Massachusetts its nickname (The Bay State) — Cape Cod. The Cape juts out into the ocean for 65 miles (105 km). At its easternmost point it hooks north, cupping the side of the state like a hand. Its offshore waters are among the most treacherous in the country.

New England Upland

West of the Coastal Lowlands is the New England Upland, a hilly region stretching from New Jersey to Maine. In Massachusetts it is split in two sections: the Connecticut River Valley and the Berkshires.

Connecticut River Valley

The Connecticut River flows through the Uplands. It forms much of the boundary between Vermont and New Hampshire, then moves south through Massachusetts and Connecticut to the Long Island Sound. The valley created by the river ranges between 2 and 20 miles (4.8 and 32 km) wide; the land on each side of the river is the best farmland in Massachusetts. Because of the river's deposits of silt, the soil is richer than most places in New England, which consists of the states Connecticut, Maine, Massachusetts, New Hampshire, Rhode Island, and Vermont.

The Berkshires

The far westernmost region in the state is known as the Berkshires, after the Berkshire range of mountains (some call them hills). The highest mountain in Massachusetts, Mt. Greylock (3,491 feet or 1,064 meters), is there.

The Berkshires are home to small-scale agriculture,

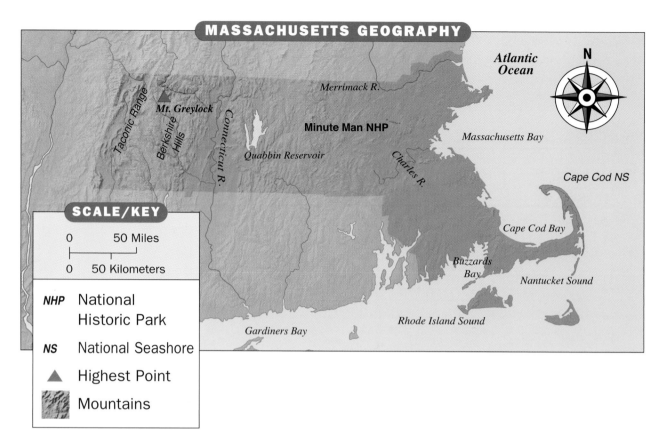

Atlantic Ocean

N

Merrimack R.

Mt. Greylock

Taconic Range

Berkshire Hills

Connecticut R.

Minute Man NHP

Massachusetts Bay

Quabbin Reservoir

Charles R.

Cape Cod NS

SCALE/KEY

| 0 | 50 Miles |
| 0 | 50 Kilometers |

Cape Cod Bay

Buzzards Bay

Nantucket Sound

NHP   National Historic Park

NS   National Seashore

▲   Highest Point

Mountains

Rhode Island Sound

Gardiners Bay

including many dairy farms. In North Adams a natural bridge of white marble has been formed by wind and melting glacers, and at nearby Sutton is a half-mile-long gorge that knifes through the rock, exposing 600 million years of geologic history.

Neighbors

Most of Massachusetts's land borders are straight lines. Vermont and New Hampshire are the state's northern neighbors; to the west is New York, and to the south are Connecticut and Rhode Island. To the east of the state is the Atlantic Ocean.

Lakes and Rivers

The land is veined with rivers — nineteen main systems, the best known of which are the Connecticut, Charles, and Merrimack. More than 1,100 ponds or lakes lie among the hills, one in almost every one of the more than 350 communities.

Although clean-up efforts have lessened pollution, many rivers and some lakes remain unfit for swimming. This has long been true of the Charles River, which separates Boston

High Points

Berkshire Hills
Mt. Greylock
3,491 feet (1,064 m)

Mt. Everett
2,624 feet (800 km)

Garnet Hill
2,178 feet (664 km)

Major Rivers

Connecticut River
407 miles
(655 km) long
60 miles (97 km) in
Massachusetts

Merrimack River
110 miles (177 km) long
50 miles (80 km) in
Massachusetts

Charles River
80 miles (130 km) long

and Cambridge, where many boaters sail and row.

Climate

Massachusetts has a temperate climate. The western part of the state is colder and snowier than the east. July is the hottest month, averaging about 71° F (21° Celsius), in contrast to 26° F (-3° C) in January. Monthly rainfall averages 3.4 inches (8.6 centimeters) in Boston and 3.7 inches (9.3 cm) in Great Barrington in the Berkshires.

Plant and Animal Life

Although the state is largely industrialized, Massachusetts has preserved many of its forests; today nearly 55 percent of the state is covered with forest. Three national wildlife refuges and the Cape Cod National Seashore enable contact with nature.

The most common trees in Massachusetts are ash, beech, birch, hemlock, maple, pine, and oak. Although pines and hemlocks are conifers (evergreens), the other trees are deciduous and lose their leaves each fall after turning orange, yellow, and red. Native flowers include trilliums and violets, as well as flowering trees and bushes such as dogwoods and azaleas.

The Coastal Lowland's ecosystem is not like that of the rest of the state. There, tufts of grass spring up along the sand dunes, and gnarled jack pines and scrub oaks, some only a few feet high, grow in bunches.

Few large animals other than deer remain in the wild, but there are still some bear and moose in the western part of the state. Other animals in the woods include deer, beaver, muskrat, mink, otter, snowshoe hare, red fox, woodchuck, raccoon, and chipmunk.

Along the shores sandpipers, blue herons, American egrets, sanderlings, and turnstones can be seen. Water birds include gulls, scoters, cormorants, and loons; most often seen on land are kingfishers, warblers, bobwhites, brown thrashers, pheasants, sparrow hawks, yellow-shafted flickers, and whippoorwills.

Average January temperature range
Boston 28.8°F (-1.8°C)
Great Barrington 20.1°F (-6.6°C)

Average July temperature range
Boston 73.4°F (23°C)
Great Barrington 68°F (20°C)

Average yearly rainfall
Boston 38 inches (96.5 cm)
Great Barrington 48.8 inches (123.9 cm)

Average yearly snowfall
Boston 40 inches (107 cm)
Great Barrington 70 inches (178 cm)

▼ Ring-necked pheasants live on a diet of insects and berries. Their nesting time varies among the different regions of the United States. Massachusetts's ring-necked pheasants nest in May.

Industry to Internet

> There is a certain proportionate Quantity of Money requisite to carry on the Trade of a Country freely and currently; More than which would be of no Advantage in Trade, and Less, if much less, exceedingly detrimental to it...
>
> — *Benjamin Franklin, A Modest Enquiry into the Nature and Necessity of Paper Currency (1729)*

The economy of Massachusetts today is based on technology, service industries, and tourism. This is fairly new for Massachusetts. In the seventeenth and eighteenth centuries the state's economy was farming-based, and in the nineteenth and much of the twentieth centuries, the economy was mostly based on manufacturing.

Foreign trade, fishing, and agriculture were the economy's first mainstays. Sailors brought exotic goods from China, the West Indies, and other faraway lands. Fishing was lucrative, adventuresome, and dangerous — more than ten thousand Gloucester fishermen have lost their lives over the centuries.

Fishing and shipbuilding went hand in hand. Between 1789 and 1810 the Massachusetts fleet grew tenfold, and many ships fought against the British and French on the high seas. At the height of the whaling boom in the nineteenth century, 329 whaling vessels sailed from New Bedford, in addition to others from Nantucket Island and other ports, bringing in $10,000,000 worth of cargo each year in their holds.

Whaling did not last, and even fishing had a slump in the 1960s due to overfishing. By the late 1970s, however, the industry had made a comeback, and Massachusetts ranks among the top four U.S. states in value of fish landings.

The state's main cash crop is cranberries; the purple sandy bogs of southeastern Massachusetts and Cape Cod produce about 50 percent of the U.S. cranberry supply. Greenhouse

Top Employers
(of workers age sixteen and over)

Service	36%
Wholesale and retail trade	20%
Manufacturing	18%
Finance, insurance, and real estate	8%
Transportation and public utilities	6%
Construction	5.4%
Agriculture	1%

DID YOU KNOW?

Among the most impressive feats of early railroad building was the 4.5-mile (7.24-km) Hoosac Tunnel, drilled under the Hoosac Mountain Range in northwestern Massachusetts between 1851 and 1875.

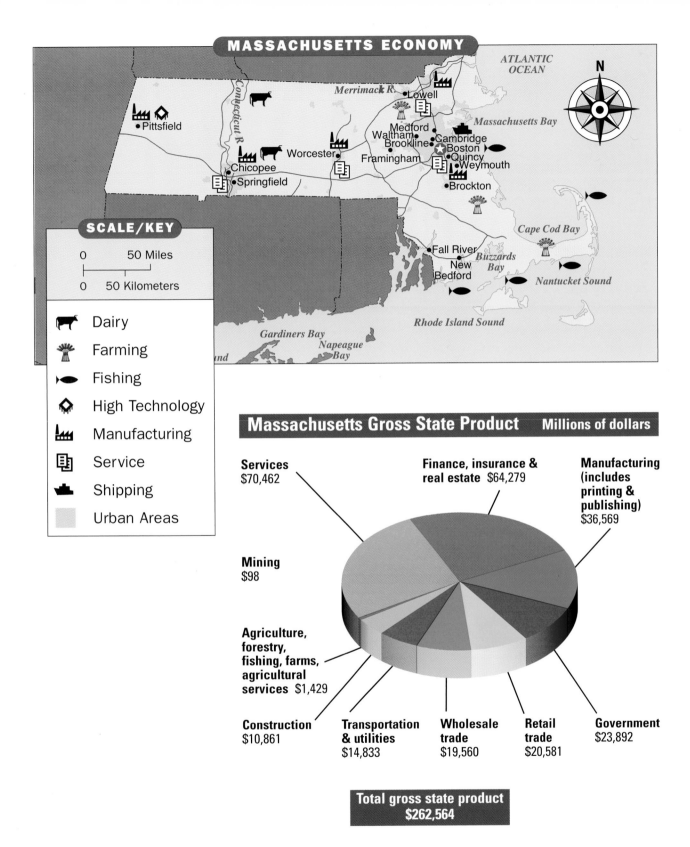

MASSACHUSETTS ECONOMY

ATLANTIC OCEAN

N

Merrimack R.
• Lowell

Massachusetts Bay

Pittsfield •

Medford
Waltham
Brookline
Worcester •
Cambridge
• Boston
Framingham
Quincy
• Weymouth

Chicopee •
• Springfield

• Brockton

Cape Cod Bay

• Fall River
New Bedford
Buzzards Bay

Nantucket Sound

Rhode Island Sound

Gardiners Bay
Napeague Bay

SCALE/KEY

0   50 Miles

0   50 Kilometers

- Dairy
- Farming
- Fishing
- High Technology
- Manufacturing
- Service
- Shipping
- Urban Areas

Massachusetts Gross State Product   Millions of dollars

Services $70,462

Finance, insurance & real estate $64,279

Manufacturing (includes printing & publishing) $36,569

Mining $98

Agriculture, forestry, fishing, farms, agricultural services $1,429

Construction $10,861

Transportation & utilities $14,833

Wholesale trade $19,560

Retail trade $20,581

Government $23,892

Total gross state product $262,564

Source: U.S. Department of Commerce, Bureau of Economic Analysis, Regional Economic Analysis Division

and nursery products are the main source of farm income, followed by dairy products.

Copper and iron were once mined in Massachusetts, but mineral production is currently limited to sand, gravel, stone, and clay.

Manufacturing

Manufacturing in Massachusetts began in the mid-1600s, when John Winthrop, Jr. (the son of Governor Winthrop) opened an ironworks and a salt factory.

Textile manufacturing mills became a major part of the state's economy when Lowell built his first power loom. But working conditions in the mills were dangerous; the air was filled with lint, machinery was deafeningly noisy, and wages were so low that families could barely afford to eat, even when both parents and children worked.

In 1912 new laws shortened the workweek, which cut pay for factory workers. Workers in Lawrence went on strike for two months and won a small pay raise. One striker carried a banner that said, "We want bread, but we want roses, too." The incident is known as the "Bread and Roses" strike.

As we go marching, marching, we bring the greater days,
The rising of the women means the rising of the race.
No more the drudge and idler, ten that toil where one reposes,
But a sharing of life's glories: Bread and roses, bread and roses.

▲ Fishing is a major industry in Massachusetts.

▼ Massachusetts was home to many of the nation's first factories. In this undated photo, thousands of factory employees gather for a group shot.

*Our lives shall not be sweated from birth until life closes;
hearts starve as well as bodies; bread and roses,
bread and roses.*
— James Oppenheim, 1912

In its early years Massachusetts was known for producing a wide variety of goods. One of the first shoe plants in America was in Beverly; watch-making plants opened in Waltham, Salem, and Boston. Massachusetts also produced rocking chairs (Gardner), leather (Peabody), knives and tools (Greenfield), paper and envelopes (Worcester), and shovels (made in North Eaton and used by the forty-niners during the California gold rush).

▲ Massachusetts is famous for its cranberry crop.

International Airport		
Airport	Location	Passengers per year (2000)
Logan International Airport	Boston	27,412,926

The Late Twentieth Century

After World War II the computer and technology industries provided a much-needed boost to the state's economy. Lynn's General Electric plant began producing the first U.S. jet engine in 1942; scientists at the Massachusetts Institute of Technology (MIT) in Cambridge teamed up with the army to design and build computers.

The suburbs of Boston have become known for their research-and-development facilities, which have contributed to computer technology. In the last few years of the twentieth century, the "new economy" of technology and the Internet brought an economic boom to the western part of the state, too. Internet start-up companies often settled in the abandoned mills of an earlier economic revolution.

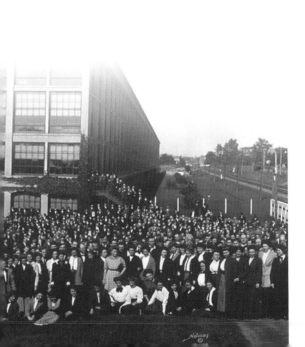

The Common Good

> Puritanism, believing itself quick with the seed of religious liberty, laid, without knowing it, the egg of democracy.
>
> — *James Russell Lowell*

Beginning with the Mayflower Compact, drawn up by the Pilgrims in 1620, Massachusetts has always valued the idea of government by the people, for the people. At that time the concept of "the divine right of kings" dominated Europe. Many people believed that God had given kings the right to rule. The idea of self-government by the people was almost unknown.

Massachusetts is officially not a state, but a commonwealth. The word comes from the Old English *commonweal*, which means "the common welfare." It appealed to the state's founders because it suggested a government of the people, for the common good of the people — just like the Mayflower Compact.

Like the government of the United States, the Massachusetts state government is divided into three branches: executive, judicial, and legislative.

The Executive Branch

The head of Massachusetts's executive branch is the governor. He or she is elected for four years and can only serve two consecutive terms within a twelve-year period. The governor serves as the state's chief executive officer and also as the commander in chief of Massachusetts's military branches. As the elected political

DID YOU KNOW?

Three other states — Virginia, Pennsylvania, and Kentucky — are also commonwealths.

Posts in the Executive Branch		
Office	**Length of Term**	**Term Limits**
Governor	4 years	2 consecutive terms in 12 years
Lieutenant Governor	4 years	None
Secretary of the Commonwealth	4 years	None
Attorney General	4 years	None
State Auditor	4 years	None
Treasurer and Receiver General	4 years	None

head of the state, the governor can grant pardons to convicted criminals (on the advice of a special executive council), distribute the state's budget, and accept or veto the bills passed by the legislature. Other positions in the executive branch include the lieutenant governor, the secretary of the commonwealth, the treasurer and receiver general, the state auditor, and the attorney general.

The Legislative Branch

The Massachusetts Great and General Court, today called the General Court, has been around since the days of John Winthrop, the first leader of the Massachusetts Bay Colony. In those days, Massachusetts was a part of England, but because it was so far away it was allowed basically to run itself, which laid the foundation for the commonwealth's history of self-government.

The legislature began as a one-house entity but became *bicameral* (has two houses) in 1644. The two houses of the Massachusetts legislature are the House of Representatives and the Senate. Back then the House consisted of two deputies elected from each town — and since there were not very many towns, it was a small legislative body. Today there are 160 members of the House of Representatives.

After independence was declared, the General Court drew up a constitution for what was then called the State of Massachusetts Bay. It was rejected by the people of Massachusetts, in part because it was not drafted by elected representatives of the people. In 1779 a new convention, one with elected representatives, was convened in Cambridge. John Adams was the main author of the new constitution of the Commonwealth of Massachusetts, which was ratified in 1780.

Many of the details that John Adams and his compatriots wrote into the Massachusetts constitution inspired the federal constitution. Today Massachusetts is the only one of the thirteen original colonies that still

▼ The state capitol building in Boston was built in 1789 and is now part museum.

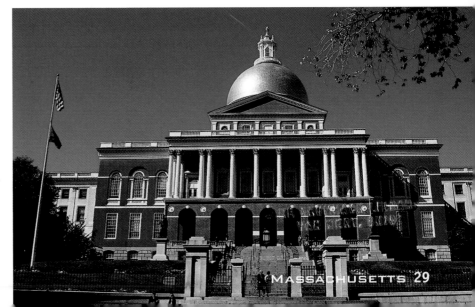

uses its first constitution. It has been amended, or changed, many times, however, and its original authors might not recognize it today.

In October of 1780 the General Court of the Commonwealth of Massachusetts met for the first time as the legislative branch of the new state's government. It was exactly 150 years after the first meeting of John Winthrop's Great and General Court. Today the legislature consists of 40 senators and 160 representatives.

▲ Inside the State House Hall in Boston.

The legislative process in Massachusetts is unique in many ways. In Massachusetts legislation may be introduced by citizen petitions, and most legislative proposals have public hearings.

The Judicial Branch

The state's judicial branch is divided into three levels: the Supreme Judicial Court, the highest court in the state; the Appeals Court; and a number of different trial courts that handle civil and criminal trials. Justices are appointed by the governor, with the advice and consent of the governor's executive council.

Local Government

Another aspect of Massachusetts government that is unusual is the town meeting. The first recorded town meeting took place in Dorchester in 1633, when citizens were summoned by the sound of a drum. A year later Charlestown organized the first Board of Selectmen, a local government intended to balance the power of the colony's executive. Today some Massachusetts towns are run by Boards of Selectmen (an official term — the boards are made up of men and women) rather than by mayors.

Thanks to the 1966 Home Rule Amendment, towns can

General Court			
House	Number of Members	Length of Term	Term Limits
Senate	40 senators	4 years	2 Terms
House of Representatives	160 representatives	2 years	2 Terms

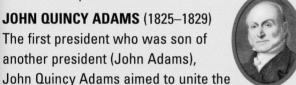

The White House via Massachusetts

Five Bay Staters have served as President of the United States — though not all were state residents when elected.

JOHN ADAMS (1797–1801)

President Adams negotiated Jay's Treaty of 1794, which gave certain trading rights to England so the British would stop attacking American ships that traded with France. He also signed into law the Alien and Sedition Acts, which limited free speech.

JOHN QUINCY ADAMS (1825–1829)
The first president who was son of another president (John Adams), John Quincy Adams aimed to unite the nation with a series of highways and canals. He also wanted to establish a national university, pay for scientific expeditions, and build a national observatory. In 1830 he joined the House of Representatives, where he campaigned in favor of preserving civil liberties.

CALVIN COOLIDGE (1923–1929)
He was known for having a "talent for doing nothing." Since the country was prosperous during his term, he did little to change things. He was also known for communicating a lot with very few words.

JOHN F. KENNEDY (1961–1963)
The first citizen of Irish Catholic descent to be elected to the office of president, he fought hard for equal rights, calling for new civil rights legislation. Kennedy was mourned by the nation when he was assassinated (on November 22, 1963) after barely one thousand days in office.

GEORGE H. W. BUSH (1989–1993) During President Bush's term, the Berlin Wall fell. He is remembered for foreign policy decisions such as sending American troops into Panama to overthrow General Manuel Noriega and for defeating Iraq in the Persian Gulf War.

change their government without the permission of the state legislature. Today town meetings are still called in many towns in Massachusetts — sometimes to settle quarrels, sometimes to discuss important local issues about roads and schools, and sometimes just because they're a fun way for the participants to be together and involve themselves in local government.

Political History

In the 1840s and 1850s there was a large Irish immigration into the state; most of these immigrants affiliated with the Democratic Party, which helped the party come into prominence. Today the Democratic Party dominates the political landscape in Massachusetts.

DID YOU KNOW?
The Massachusetts Constitution is the oldest governing constitution in the world.

Massachusetts Mecca

> Where the heart is, there the muses, there the gods sojourn, and not in any geography of fame. Massachusetts, Connecticut River, and Boston Bay, you think paltry places, and the ear loves names of foreign and classic topography. But here we are; and, if we tarry a little, we may come to learn that here is best. See to it, only, that thyself is here; — and art and nature, hope and fate, friends, angels, and the Supreme Being, shall not absent from the chamber where thou sittest.
>
> — *Ralph Waldo Emerson, "Heroism," 1841*

The arts have long flourished in Massachusetts. In its earliest years, the state was a literary mecca during the "American Renaissance," beginning around the time of the Revolution and lasting through most of the nineteenth century. Today it is home to orchestras, theater companies, pop musicians, and museums.

Literary Arts

Massachusetts writers helped create the foundation of American literature; these writers included Ralph Waldo Emerson, Henry David Thoreau, Nathaniel Hawthorne, and Louisa May Alcott, all of whom were neighbors. Hawthorne enjoyed writing in Pittsfield, in the Berkshires; so did Herman Melville, Oliver Wendell Holmes, and Henry Wadsworth Longfellow. Among other famous writers of the era were John Greenleaf Whittier and James Russell Lowell, as well as Emily Dickinson, the "Belle of Amherst," today generally considered one of the great U.S. poets of the nineteenth century.

▲ Henry Wadsworth Longfellow.

Music and Theater

The Boston Symphony Orchestra is generally regarded as one of the finest musical ensembles in the world. Since 1938 the orchestra has spent summers performing at Tanglewood, in the town of Lenox. Other Berkshire summer

festivals include Jacob's Pillow Dance Festival (Becket), the Williamstown Theatre Festival (Williamstown), and the Berkshire Theatre Festival (Sheffield). The large number of cultural events that take place in the Berkshires each summer is a testament to the region as a summer retreat. While in the Berkshires visitors can explore the Appalachian Trail, which winds its way through this section of the state. The Appalachian Trail stretches from Maine to Georgia.

Boston is known for its Arts in the Parks series (concerts and programs presented on the banks of the Charles River), as well as for having a vibrant Irish-American music scene. Rock band Aerosmith came from Boston, as did ska band The Mighty Mighty Bosstones. The live music scene isn't only to be found in Boston; Northampton, in the Connecticut River Valley region, is home to the Iron Horse Music Hall, one of the nation's best spots for live folk, pop, and world music concerts.

Museums

The state's museums appeal to a variety of interests. Boston is home to the Museum of Fine Arts, the Computer Museum, and the John F. Kennedy Library and Museum, as well as the Museum of Science, the New England Aquarium, and the Children's Museum, which pioneered the use of participatory exhibits. The western part of the state is home to museums, too; the Sterling and Francine Clark Art Institute (Williamstown) is known for its Impressionist collection, and the Massachusetts Museum of Contemporary Art (North Adams) is one of the largest contemporary art museums in the world.

Education

Of the 257 colleges and universities in New England, 118 are in Massachusetts. Education lies close to the heart of Massachusetts's social and cultural life.

Harvard College (now Harvard University) was founded in 1636 in New Towne (now Cambridge). Although it was designed to provide the colony with a supply of trained clergy, its graduates became community leaders and helped to provide schooling throughout the colony. In 1647 towns with fifty householders were required to support an elementary school; those with one hundred, an elementary and a secondary school.

In the 1800s Massachusetts became a pioneer in kindergarten and secondary education. A state public school system was developed in 1840. Today the state has many private high schools ("prep schools") of national ranking. Roxbury Latin School, founded in 1645, is among the nation's oldest.

From Sprague to MASS MoCA

In 1941 the Sprague Electric Company moved into its "Brown Street" facility in North Adams. Over the next forty-five years, the 153,000-square-foot (14,213 square meters) factory was developed into an advanced electrical products manufacturing facility. "Sprague Electric" was the heart of North Adams. Sprague physicists, chemists, electrical engineers, and technicians were called upon by the U.S. government during World War II to design and manufacture crucial components of some of its most advanced high-tech weapons systems, including the atomic bomb. The electronics business took an unexpected downturn, however, and in 1985 Sprague closed the North Adams plant. In 1999 the twenty-seven building complex reopened to the public — as the Massachusetts Museum of Contemporary Art (MASS MoCA), a "supercollider for the arts." Today the complex is a multi-disciplinary center for visual, performance, and media arts — once again, the heart of its town.

◀ The Massachusetts Institute of Technology.

Harvard is not the state's only educational star. Many of the nation's oldest and most prestigious colleges and universities are located in Massachusetts. The largest, both in Boston, are Boston University (1839) and Northeastern University (1898). Nearby are the Massachusetts Institute of Technology (Cambridge, 1861), and Tufts (Medford, 1852) and Brandeis (Waltham, 1948) universities. Amherst (Amherst, 1821) and Williams (Williamstown, 1793) colleges have perpetuated traditions of academic excellence at small schools, while Mount Holyoke (South Hadley, 1837), Wellesley (Wellesley, 1870), Smith (Northampton, 1871), and Radcliffe (Cambridge, 1879) colleges have been pioneers in women's education. Boston College (Chestnut Hill, 1863) and College of the Holy Cross (Worcester, 1843) are major Roman Catholic institutions. The University of Massachusetts (Amherst and Boston, 1863) is the principal state university.

▲ The Boston Celtics at play.

Sports

Massachusetts is home to five big-league sports teams: the Boston Red Sox (baseball), Boston Bruins (hockey), Boston Celtics (basketball), New England Revolution (soccer), and New England Patriots (football).

The Celtics have fought their way to sixteen National

Sport	Team	Home
Baseball	Boston Red Sox	Fenway Park, Boston
Basketball	Boston Celtics	Fleet Center, Boston
Football	New England Patriots	Foxboro Stadium, Foxboro
Hockey	Boston Bruins	Fleet Center, Boston
Soccer	New England Revolution	CMGI Field, Foxboro

Basketball Association (NBA) championships; they boast more title banners than any other NBA franchise. They won their last championship in 1986.

The Patriots have not won a Super Bowl but came close in the 1996 season (losing to the Green Bay Packers), and loyal fans continue to hope. Their experience is shared by Red Sox fans; the team's last championship was in 1918. Still, the Sox are legendary — Cy Young, Ted Williams, and Carl Yastrzemski are among the baseball greats who have called the Red Sox home.

Red Sox fans tell a story about Babe Ruth. Early in the baseball giant's career, the Red Sox traded him to the New York Yankees. Ever since then the team has been unable to win a championship. Fans joke that the team is under a curse for having been foolish enough to trade Babe Ruth away.

Another historic sports franchise with a spotty recent history is the Boston Bruins, who became the first National Hockey League (NHL) franchise in the United States when

▼ Fenway Park, 1914: The Boston Braves, precursors of the Milwaukee Braves and Atlanta Braves, triumph over the Philadelphia Athletics, four games to none, in the World Series.

World's Series — Braves 5 Athletics 4. 12 Innings, Fenway Park, American League Grounds, Oct. 12, 1914.

they entered the League in the 1924–25 season. The Bruins won the first of their five Stanley Cups in 1929.

The New England Revolution, a major league soccer team, is the state's newest sports team. In 2001 the team hosted its first-ever U.S. Open Cup soccer semifinal.

WGBH, Boston

In 1836 John Lowell, Jr., created the Lowell Institute, which provided the citizens of Boston with free lectures on art, science, natural history, and philosophy. Although attendance was initially high, the forum eventually became less significant in Boston public life. In the mid-1940s a Harvard professor suggested that the lectures be broadcast to the public via radio. The Lowell Institute Cooperative Broadcasting Council (LICBC) was formed.

Unable to get reliable airtime on local stations, the LICBC received a license to operate its own radio station in 1950. In 1967 Congress passed the Public Broadcasting Act and established the Corporation for Public Broadcasting. That same year WGBH television was born.

Today WGBH produces critically acclaimed television shows for stations around the country. Recently it has begun dramatizing U.S. works of literature for viewing on *Masterpiece Theater*, as well as continuing to create favorite programs for kids including *Arthur*, *Where in Time Is Carmen Sandiego?*, and *Zoom*.

▲ **Legendary Red Sox pitcher Cy Young.**

DID YOU KNOW?

The "GBH" in WGBH's call letters stand for "Great Blue Hill," the name of the hill on which the station's transmitter stands.

From Politicians to Poets

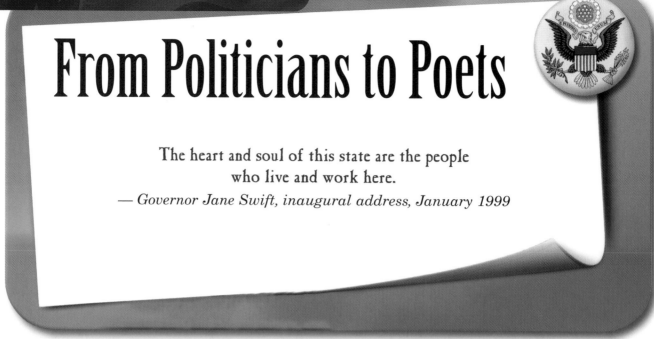

The heart and soul of this state are the people
who live and work here.

— *Governor Jane Swift, inaugural address, January 1999*

Following are only a few of the thousands of people who lived, died, or spent most of their lives in Massachusetts and made extraordinary contributions to the state and the nation.

MASSASOIT
NATIVE AMERICAN LEADER
BORN: *circa 1590, near present-day Bristol, RI*
DIED: *circa September, 1661, near present-day Bristol, RI*

A chief of the Wampanoag, Massasoit (also known as Ousamequin, or "yellow feather") established peace among all the Wampanoag tribes and the English settlers of Plymouth Colony with the Peace Treaty of March 22, 1621. In that year he traveled with his friend Samoset to the Pilgrims' colony at Plymouth. Massasoit taught the settlers how to plant, fish, and cook in the New World. When he became sick in 1623, then-Governor Edward Winslow traveled through a snowstorm to minister to him. The peace he established lasted his entire lifetime.

SAMUEL ADAMS
POLITICIAN
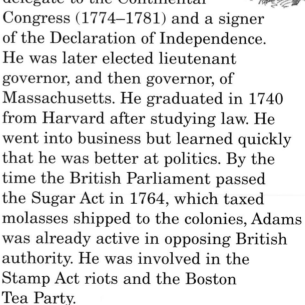
BORN: *September 27, 1722, Boston*
DIED: *October 3, 1803, Boston*

Samuel Adams was a delegate to the Continental Congress (1774–1781) and a signer of the Declaration of Independence. He was later elected lieutenant governor, and then governor, of Massachusetts. He graduated in 1740 from Harvard after studying law. He went into business but learned quickly that he was better at politics. By the time the British Parliament passed the Sugar Act in 1764, which taxed molasses shipped to the colonies, Adams was already active in opposing British authority. He was involved in the Stamp Act riots and the Boston Tea Party.

John Adams

BORN: *October 30, 1735, Braintree (Quincy)*
DIED: *July 4, 1826, Quincy*

John Adams graduated from Harvard College in 1755. He later moved to Boston to become a leading attorney in the Massachusetts colony. Adams wrote resolutions against the Stamp Act and represented Massachusetts at the First and Second Continental Congresses. He was a strong supporter of the colonies' complete independence from Great Britain. During the Revolutionary War, Adams was sent to Europe to help Benjamin Franklin strengthen ties with France and other European countries. At the end of the war, he helped negotiate the Treaty of Paris. In 1788, Adams was elected to the vice presidency and served two terms under George Washington before becoming the second president of the United States in 1797. He was the first president to live in the White House. One year before he died, Adams's eldest son became the sixth president.

Phyllis Wheatley
POET

BORN: *circa 1753, present-day Senegal, West Africa*
DIED: *Dec. 5, 1784, Boston*

Phyllis (also spelled Phillis) Wheatley was the first female African-American poet of note in the United States. She was brought to Boston on a slave ship in 1761, when she was about eight years old. John Wheatley, a tailor, bought her to serve his wife. The Wheatleys educated Phyllis (not an ordinary act at that time), and she mastered English in less than two years. She also learned Greek and Latin. She was escorted by Mr. Wheatley's son to London in 1773; there her first book, *Poems on Various Subjects, Religious and Moral,* was published. Both Mr. and Mrs. Wheatley died soon thereafter, and Wheatley was freed. In 1778 she married John Peters, who eventually abandoned her. At the end of her life, Wheatley was working as a servant; she died in poverty.

Henry David Thoreau
PHILOSOPHER

BORN: *July 12, 1817, Concord*
DIED: *May 6, 1862, Concord*

Henry David Thoreau was an essayist, poet, and philosopher. He is best known for writing *Walden,* the chronicle of a year he spent living very simply on Walden Pond, and for his strong support of civil liberties. His most famous essay, published in 1849, is titled "Civil Disobedience."  Although widely read today, Thoreau did not enjoy financial success during his lifetime. He had to pay for the printing of his first book, *A Week on the Concord and Merrimack Rivers,* which sold only 220 copies out of a print run of roughly 900. The publishers gave the unsold copies back to him! *Walden,* the second and last of his books published during his lifetime, did slightly better but still took five years to sell two thousand copies. Today Thoreau is regarded as a classic writer because of the powerful way in which he expressed beautiful ideas.

SUSAN B. ANTHONY
SUFFRAGIST

BORN: *Feb. 15, 1820, Adams*
DIED: *March 13, 1906 , Rochester, N.Y.*

Susan B. Anthony learned to read and write when she was three years old. She was raised in the Quaker faith and eventually taught at a Quaker school. In 1849 she moved to Rochester, New York, where she met famous abolitionists and people who fought for temperance (stopping drunkenness) and women's suffrage (giving women the right to vote). She took up these causes but discovered it was difficult for a woman to be an activist because many did not take women seriously. She persisted and became a leader in many anti-slavery, pro-temperance, and pro-suffrage organizations. She cast a vote in the 1872 presidential election and was arrested and convicted immediately, but she refused to pay the fine. She died before women received the right to vote.

EMILY DICKINSON
POET

BORN: *Dec. 10, 1830, Amherst*
DIED: *May 15, 1886, Amherst*

Emily Elizabeth Dickinson, sometimes called "the New England mystic," was a lyric poet who experimented with rhythm and rhyme. Most of her poetry was only published after her death. Known also as "The Belle of Amherst," she spent most of her life in her childhood home, writing letters to a number of close friends as well as thousands of poems. The central subjects of her poems included love, death, and nature.

LOUISA MAY ALCOTT
WRITER

BORN: *Nov. 29, 1832, Germantown, PA*
DIED: *March 6, 1888, Boston*

A U.S. author known for her children's books, especially the classic *Little Women*, Louisa May Alcott spent most of her life in Boston and Concord, where she grew up in the company of Ralph Waldo Emerson, Theodore Parker, and Henry David Thoreau. Her education was largely directed by her father, first at his innovative Temple School in Boston and, later, at home. She taught briefly, worked as a housekeeper, and finally began to write. She volunteered as a nurse during the U.S. Civil War, but she contracted typhoid fever and was sent home. She never completely recovered. In 1868 she wrote the autobiographical *Little Women,* which was an immediate success.

OLIVER WENDELL HOLMES
JUDGE

BORN: *March 8, 1841, Boston*
DIED: *March 6, 1935, Washington, D.C*

Oliver Wendell Holmes was one of the best-known American judges of the 1900s. He served on the Supreme Court of the United States for nearly thirty years. As a young man in Boston, Holmes enlisted in the Union Army, fought through most of the Civil War (1861–1865), and was wounded three times. Holmes resigned as a lieutenant colonel in 1864. President Theodore Roosevelt appointed Holmes an associate justice of the Supreme Court of the United States in 1902. He disagreed so often with the majority opinions of the court that he became known as the Great Dissenter. One of his contributions was influencing judges to refrain from allowing their personal opinions to affect their decisions.

DR. SEUSS
AUTHOR AND ILLUSTRATOR

BORN: *March 2, 1904, Springfield*
DIED: *September 24, 1991, La Jolla, CA*

Theodore Geisel was born and reared in Springfield. He wrote children's books under the name "Seuss," his grandfather's last name. His first book, *And To Think That I Saw It On Mulberry Street*, was rejected by forty-three publishers! In 1954 Geisel read an article that said children were having trouble learning to read because their books were boring and used too many words. Geisel decided to try to write a book using only 250 words. The result was *The Cat In The Hat*. In 1960 a friend bet Geisel $50 that he couldn't write an entire book using only fifty words. Geisel won the bet after writing *Green Eggs and Ham*. His books, which featured rhyming text and a variety of weird and wild creatures, became national bestsellers and have been translated into more than twenty languages.

JOHN F. KENNEDY
PRESIDENT

BORN: *May 29, 1917, Brookline*
DIED: *Nov. 22, 1963, Dallas*

John F. Kennedy (JFK) was the youngest man ever elected president and the youngest to die in office. He was assassinated on

Nov. 22, 1963. Kennedy, a Democrat, was also the first Roman Catholic president. In his inaugural address President Kennedy declared that "a new generation of Americans" had taken over leadership of the country. He said Americans would ". . . pay any price, bear any burden, meet any hardship, support any friend, oppose any foe to assure the survival and the success of liberty." He told Americans, "Ask not what your country can do for you: ask what you can do for your country."

SHARON CHRISTA MCAULIFFE
TEACHER

BORN: *Sept. 2, 1948, Boston*
DIED: *Jan. 28, 1986, off Cape Canaveral, FL*

Christa McAuliffe, born Sharon Christa Corrigan, grew up in Boston. She became a teacher and taught elementary school for several years. In 1984, the National Aeronautics and Space Administration (NASA) was preparing to send the *Challenger* space shuttle into space, and they decided to send someone who was not a scientist or an astronaut. Christa McAuliffe was chosen from more than ten thousand applicants. She planned to keep a journal about her training, about the flight, and about her feelings once she returned to Earth. She was also going to teach lessons from space. Tragically, the *Challenger* exploded seventy-three seconds after lift-off. McAuliffe and the rest of the crew were killed.

Massachusetts
History At-A-Glance

1788
Massachusetts ratifies the U.S. Constitution.

1620
Pilgrims arrive on the *Mayflower* and establish Plymouth Colony.

1636
Harvard becomes the first college in the colonies.

1692
Hundreds of people are accused of witchcraft in the Salem Witch Trials.

1775
American Revolution begins in Lexington and Concord.

1797
John Adams becomes the second president of the United States.

1773
Boston Tea Party.

1647
The Massachusetts Bay Colony establishes a public education system.

1810
Francis Cabot Lowell establishes the first steam loom textile factory.

1630
Puritans establish the Massachusetts Bay Colony.

1770
Boston Massacre.

1774
The Intolerable Acts are passed.

1780
Massachusetts adopts a state constitution.

1600   **1700**   **1800**

1492
Christopher Columbus comes to the New World.

1607
Capt. John Smith and three ships land on Virginia coast and start first English settlement in New World — Jamestown.

1754–63
French and Indian War.

1776
Declaration of Independence adopted July 4.

1787
U.S. Constitution written.

1773
Boston Tea Party.

1777
Articles of Confederation adopted by Continental Congress.

1812–14
War of 1812.

United States
History At-A-Glance

▼ The Boston Red Sox line up for a team photo in 1914.

1825
John Quincy Adams of Massachusetts becomes president of the United States.

1898
The first U.S. subway system opens up in Boston.

1912
Textile mill workers strike for higher wages.

1926
The first liquid fuel rocket is launched in Auburn.

1942
The first U.S. jet engines are produced at the General Electric plant in Lynn.

1960
Senator John F. Kennedy (JFK) is elected president of the United States.

1963
JFK is assassinated.

1966
The Home Rule Amendment is passed.

1974
A federal court orders Boston to integrate its schools.

1988
Governor Michael Dukakis loses the presidential election to George H. W. Bush.

1999
Massachusetts Museum of Contemporary Art opens in the former Sprague Electric Buildings.

1800　　　**1900**　　　**2000**

1848
Gold discovered in California draws eighty thousand prospectors in the 1849 Gold Rush.

1861–65
Civil War.

1869
Transcontinental Railroad is completed.

1917–18
U.S. involvement in World War I.

1929
Stock market crash ushers in Great Depression.

1941–45
U.S. involvement in World War II.

1950–53
U.S. fights in the Korean War.

1964–73
U.S. involvement in Vietnam War.

2000
George W. Bush wins the closest presidential election in history.

2001
A terrorist attack in which four hijacked airliners crash into New York City's World Trade Center, the Pentagon, and farmland in western Pennsylvania leaves thousands dead or injured.

Festivals and Fun For All

Check web site for exact date and directions.

Boston Globe Blues and Jazz Festival, Boston

A thirty-year-old festival provides the best of blues and jazz.
www.boston.com/jazzfestival

Cider Day, Colrain

A fall cider fest complete with good food — cider, jellies, donuts, and pies.
www.ciderday.org

Great Josh Billings Runaground, Great Barrington

The oldest and largest triathlon in the United States.

Fall Foliage Festival, North Adams

Celebrate "leaf-peeping" season as the fall foliage of New England turns glorious golds and reds.
www.nberkshirechamber.com/fall

Hancock Shaker Village, Hancock

Throughout the year, this working Shaker farm offers exhibits and more.
www.hancockshakervillage.org

Harwich Cranberry Festival, Harwich

A weeklong celebration on Cape Cod of the Massachusetts state berry.
www.harwichcranberryfestival.com

Head of the Charles Regatta, Boston

More than five thousand athletes compete in the world's largest rowing regatta.
http://www.hocr.org/index2.html

Lowell Celebrates Kerouac, Lowell

The life and work of the famous author of *On the Road* is celebrated in his hometown.
www.floweringcity.org/lck

Oktoberfest at Six Flags New England, Agawam

Old World fun at New England's largest theme park.
www.sixflags.com/parks/newengland/ShowsAndEvents/list.html#Oktoberfest

Spooky World, Foxboro

During the month of October, this theme park devoted to horror provides the best in Halloween thrills and chills.
www.spookyworld.com

Thanksgiving Dinners at the Plimoth Plantation, **Plymouth**

Exhibits at the plantation include the 1627 Pilgrim Village, the Wampanoag Indian Homesite, and a replica of the *Mayflower*. The site hosts Thanksgiving Dinners complete with the original Thanksgiving menu.
www.plimoth.org

The Big E, **West Springfield**

The Eastern States Exposition is an annual fair for all of the New England states, but it's held in Massachusetts. A horse show, rides, parades, and much, much more.
www.thebige.com

The Boston Tea Party, **Boston**

Dress up as a Revolutionary Rebel disguised as a Native American and plunder the *Beaver II,* a working replica of one of the original Tea Party ships.
www.bostonteapartyship.com

The Boston Marathon, **Boston**

The first Boston Marathon was held in 1897. Today thousands go to see the entrants race.
www.bostonmarathon.org

▼ **The Boston Marathon, held on or around Patriots Day, April 19.**

Books

Erickson, Paul. *Daily Life in the Pilgrim Colony* 1636. New York: Clarion Books, 2001. What life was like in Massachusetts almost four hundred years ago.

Forten, Charlotte L, Christy Steele (Editor), Suzanne L. Bunkers, and Kerry Graves (Editor). *Free Black Girl Before the Civil War: The Diary of Charlotte Forten,* 1854. Mankato, MN: Blue Earth Books, 1999. Read the diary of an African-American girl who lived in Massachusetts before the Civil War.

Millender, Dharathula H. and Gray Morrow. *Crispus Attucks: Black Leader of Colonial Patriots.* New York: Aladdin Paperbacks, 1986. Crispus Attucks was killed in the Boston Massacre, one of the events that started the Revolutionary War.

Peters, Russell M. and John Madama. *Clambake: A Wampanoag Tradition.* Danbury, CT: Children's Press, 1998. Native American traditions in Massachusetts that link the past to the present.

Pletcher, Larry B. *It Happened in Massachusetts.* Helena, MT: TwoDot Books, 1999. The stories behind the stories in Massachusetts history.

Web Sites

▶ Official state Web site
www.state.ma.us

▶ Official capital Web site
www.ci.boston.ma.us

▶ The Freedom Trail: take a virtual tour of the road to freedom
www.thefreedomtrail.org

▶ The Salem Witch Trials: All the facts about Salem's 1692 witch hunts
www.salemwitchmuseum.com

▶ Paul Revere's historic house museum: Take a virtual walk-through tour
www.paulreverehouse.org

▶ Living History Museum: 17th Century Plymouth
www.plimoth.org

Films and Documentaries

Shearer, Jacqueline. *The MA 54th Colored Infantry,* WGBH Boston, 1998. Learn about the brave African Americans from Massachusetts who fought in the Civil War.

Note: Page numbers in *italics* refer to illustrations or photographs.

A

abolition, 15, 39
Adams, John, 13, 29, *31*
Adams, John Quincy, *31*, 39
Adams, Samuel, 12, 13, *38*
Aerosmith, 33
African-Americans, 12, 15, 39, 46
age distribution, 16
agriculture, 24, 25–26, *27*
airports, 27
Alcott, Louisa May, 40
Algonquian, 8
Anthony, Susan B., 39
Appalachian Trail, 33
Arbella (ship), 10
area, 6, 20
Arts in the Parks, 33
Assembly Hall, *30*
attractions
    Appalachian Trail, 33
    Boston Marathon, *45*
    Cape Cod, 7, 20, *20*, 21, 23
    festivals, 44–45
    lakes, 20, 21, 22
    mountains, 7, *9*, 21, *21*, 22
    museums, *29*, 32–34
    music, 32, 33
    rivers, 13, *18*, 22
    sports, *14*, 35, 35–37
Attucks, Crispus, 12

B

Back Bay, 4
baseball, *14*, 35–37
basketball, 35–37
Battle of Bunker Hill, *12*, 13
"Belle of Amherst, The," 40, *40*
Berkshires, *9*, 20, 21, 22
berry (state), 6
beverage (state), 6
Beverly, 27
Beverly Pond, *20*
Big E, the, 45
Billings Landing, *7*
bird (state), 6
books about Massachusetts, 46
Boston, 4, 6, *18*, *29*
Boston Braves, *36–37*
Boston Bruins, 35, 36–37
Boston Celtics, *35*, 35–36
Boston Common, 15
Boston Globe Blues and Jazz Festival, 44
Boston Marathon, *45*
Boston Massacre, 12
Boston Red Sox, 35, 36, *42–43*

Boston Symphony Orchestra, 32
Boston Tea Party, 12, *13*, 45
boycotts, 12–13
Bradford, William, 9–10
"Bread and Roses" strike, 26–27
British East India Company, 12
British Parliament, 11
Bush, George H., *31*

C

Cape Ann, *5*
Cape Cod, 7, 20, *20*, 21, 23
capital, 6
capitol building, *29*
Cat in the Hat, The, (Dr. Seuss), 40
cat (state), 6
Champlain, Samuel de, 8
Charles River, 13, *18*, 22
Christianity, 19
Cider Day, 44
cities, *5*
"Civil Disobedience" (Thoreau), 39
Civil Rights Movement, 15
Civil War, 15
Clambake: A Wampanoag Tradition (Peters), 46
climate, 8, 23
Coastal Lowlands, 20–21, 23
coastal towns, *5*
coastline, 20
colleges, 14, 34–35
commonwealths, 28
computer industry, 27
Concord, 7, 13
Connecticut River, 22
Connecticut River Valley, 20, 21
constitution, 29–30, 31
Continental Congress, 12–13
cookies, 6, *7*
Coolidge, Calvin, *31*
Corporation for Public Broadcasting, 37
courts, 30
cranberries, 24, *27*, 44
Crispus Attucks: Black Leader of Colonial Patriots (Millender), 46
cultural events, 32–33

D

Daily Life in the Pilgrim Colony (Erickson), 46
Dawes, William, 13
Daye, Stephen, 7
Declaration of Independence, 13
Democratic Party, 31
dessert (state), 6

Dickinson, Emily, 32, *40*
documentaries about Massachusetts, 46
dog (state), 6
Dr. Seuss, 40–41
Durand, Asher Brown, *9*

E

economy and commerce, 4, 11, 14, 16, 24–27, *25*, *26*
    "Triangle Trade," 11
education, 4, 14, 15, *18*, 19, 34–35
electronics industry, 34
Emerson, Ralph Waldo, 32
employers, 24
English community, 16, 17–18
Eriksson, Leif, 8
ethnic makeup of Massachusetts, *16*, 16–19, *17*, *19*
executive branch, *28*, 28–29

F

factories, *26*
Fall Foliage Festival, 44
farming, 24, 25–26, *27*
Fenway Park, *36–37*
festivals, *19*, 44–45
54th Massachusetts Volunteer Infantry, 15
54th Regiment Memorial, 15
Fig Newtons, 7
films about Massachusetts, 46
fish and fishing, 6, 24, *26*
flower (state), 6
football, 35–37
Franklin, Benjamin, 13, 24
Free Black Girl Before the Civil War: The Diary of Charlotte Forten (Forten), 46
Freedom Trail, the, 7

G

game bird (state), 6
Garnet Hill, 22
Garrison, William Lloyd, 14–15
Geisel, Theodore, 40–41
General Assembly, *30*
General Court of the Commonwealth of Massachusetts, 30
General Electric, 27
geography of Massachusetts, 4–5, 20–23
Great Depression, 15
"Great Dissenter, The " (Holmes), 40
Great Josh Billings Runaground, 44

Green Eggs and Ham (Dr. Seuss), 41
gross state product, *25*

H

Hancock, John, 11
Hancock Shaker Village, 44
Harvard University, 4, 34–35
Harwich Cranberry Festival, 44
Head of the Charles Regatta, 44
high-tech industry, 27
hockey, 35–37
Holmes, Oliver Wendell, 40
Home Rule Amendment, 31
Hoosac Tunnel, 24
House of Representatives, 29, *30*
Hutchinson, Deborah, 20

I

immigration, *16*, 16–19
Industrial Revolution, 4, 14, 16
industry, 4, 14, 16, 24, 26–27, 34. *See also* economy and commerce
insect (state), 6
Intolerable Acts, 11–12
Irish community, 16–18, 33
It Happened in Massachusetts (Pletcher), 46
Italian community, 17–18

J

Jackson, Joseph, 11
John F. Kennedy Library and Museum, *33*
judicial branch, 30

K

Kennedy, John F., *31*, *33*, 41
Kennedy Biscuit Works, 7

L

labor disputes, 26
Lake Chargoggagoggmanchaugg-agoggchaubunagunga-maugg, 20
lakes, 20, 21, 22
legislative branch, 29–30
Lexington, 7, 13
The Liberator, 15
literary arts, 32
Little Women (Alcott), 40
local government, 30–31
Logan International Airport, 27
Longfellow, Henry Wadsworth, 13, *32*
Lowell, Francis Cabot, 14
Lowell, James Russell, 28

Lowell, John, Jr., 37
Lowell, Massachusetts, 6
Lowell Celebrates Kerouac, 44
Lowell Institute Cooperative
   Broadcasting Council
   (LICBC), 37
Loyalists, 13

M
manufacturing, 14–15, *26,*
   26–27
maps of Massachusetts, *5,*
   22, 25
Massachuset Indians, 8
Massachusetts Bay Colony, 10
Massachusetts Institute
   of Technology (MIT), 7,
   27, *34*
Massachusetts Museum of
   Contemporary Art (MASS
   MoCA), 34
Massasoit, 10, 38
Mayflower Compact, 9–10, 28
Mayflower (ship), 9–10, *10*
McAuliffe, Sharon Christa, 41
Merrimack River, 22
Mighty Mighty Bosstones, 33
Mohican Indians, 8
Monument Mountain, *9*
motto (state), 6
Mount Everett, 22
Mount Greylock, 21, *21,* 22
Mount Greylock State
   Reservation, 7
Mount Holyoke College, 14,
   14, 35
mountains, 7, *9,* 21, *21,* 22
muffin (state), 6
museums, *29,* 33–34
music, 32, 33

N
naming of Massachusetts, 8
National Aeronautics and
   Space Administration
   (NASA), 41
National Association for the
   Advancement of Colored
   People (NAACP), 15
National Biscuit Company
   (Nabisco), 7
Native Americans, 8, 10, 19, 38
Nauset Indians, 8
New England Patriots, 35, 36
New England Revolution,
   35, 37
New England Upland, 20, 21
newspapers, 10

nickname of Massachusetts,
   4, 21
Nimoy, Leonard, 41
Nipmuc Indians, 8

O
Oktoberfest at Six Flags,
   New England, 44
Oppenheim, James, 27

P
Pemberton, Samuel, 11
Pennacook Indians, 8
Pilgrims, 4, 8, 10
plant life, 23
Plum Island National Wildlife
   Refuge, *20*
Plymouth Rock, *7*
Pocumtuc Indians, 8
politics and poitcal figures
   Adams, John, 13, 29, *31,* 38
   Adams, John Quincy, *31*
   Adams, Samuel, 12, 13, *38*
   Anthony, Susan B., 39
   Boston Tea Party, 12, *13,*
   45
   boycotts, 12–13
   Bradford, William, 9–10
   branches of government,
   28–30
   Bush, George H., *31*
   Continental Congress,
   12–13
   Coolidge, Calvin, *31*
   Democratic Party, 31
   Hancock, John, 11
   Holmes, Oliver
   Wendell, 40
   Home Rule Amendment,
   31
   Intolerable Acts, 11–12
   Kennedy, John F., *31,*
   33, 41
   local government, 30–31
   Mayflower Compact,
   9–10, 28
   John Smith, 9
   Tories, 13
George Washington, 11
population, 6, 16–19
prep schools, 34
presidents from
   Massachusetts, *31, 41*
printing press, 7
Protestantism, 19
Public Broadcasting Act, 37
Publick Occurrences both
   Forreign and Domestick

(newspaper), 10
Puritans, 4, 10, 19

Q
Quabbin Reservoir, 21
Quakers, 39
Quincy Market, *17*

R
radio, 37
railroads, 24
rainfall, 23
religion, 19
Revere, Paul, 13
Revolutionary War, 4, 7, 11
rivers, 13, *18,* 22
Robert Gould Shaw
   Memorial, 15
Roman Catholicism, 19
Rowe, John, 11
Roxbury Latin School, 34
Ruddock, John, 11
Ruth, Babe, 36

S
Samson, Deborah, 11
schools, 15
Schwarzman, Beth, 20
seal of Massachusetts, 28
Senate, 29, *30*
Separatists, 9–10
Shaw, Robert Gould, 15
shipbuilding industry, 24
Shurtleff, Robert, 11
slavery, 14–15
Smith, John, 9
snowfall, 23
soccer, 35–37
song (state), 6
Spock (Leonard Nimoy), 41
Spooky World, 44
sports, *14, 35,* 35–37
Sprague Electric Company, 34
Springfield, Massachusetts, 6
Stamp Act, 11
Stanley, Francis, 15
Stanley, Freelan, 15
Stanley Steamer, 15
Star Trek, 41
State Heroine of
   Massachusetts, 11
state symbols, 6
statehood, 6
Sterling, Massachusetts, 7
Sterling and Francine Clark
   Art Institute, 34
strikes, 26
Sturbridge Village, *21*

suburbs, 27
Sugar Act, 11
Supreme Court justices, 40
Swift, Jane, 38
Swift River Valley, 21

T
Tanglewood, 32
technology industry, 27
temperance movement, 39
temperature, 23
textile industry, 14, 26
Thanksgiving, 4, 10, 45
Thoreau, Henry David, 39, *39*
timeline of Massachusetts
   history, *42–43*
Tories, 13
tourism. *See* attractions
Treaty of Paris, 13
trees of Massachusetts, 6, 23
"Triangle Trade," 11
Tyler, Mary Sawyer, 7

U
universities, 34–35
U.S. Constitution, 13

W
Walden (Thoreau), 39
Wampanoag Indians, 8, 10, 38
Washington, George, 11
waterways, *5. See also* rivers
web sites about
   Massachusetts, 46
Week on the Concorde and
   Merrimack Rivers
   (Thoreau), 39
Wellesley, Massachusetts, 7
WGBH, Boston, 37
whaling industry, 24
Wheatley, Phyllis, 39
wildlife, *21,* 23, *23*
Wilson, Woodrow, 16
Winthrop, John, 10, 29
Winthrop, John, Jr., 26
Women's Rights Convention,
   15
women's suffrage, 15, 39
Worcester, Massachusetts, 6
World War II, 15, 34

Y
Yastrzemski, Carl, 36
Young, Cy, 36, *37*